UNGODLY

Ungodly

MAGGIE BOWYER

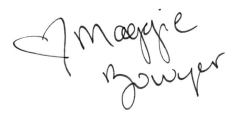

Margaret Bowyer

For the man who has supported me as I search for the missing pieces of myself; for the family that has held me in my most broken moments; for everyone at College Park Baptist Church who showed me true, godly love.

There may be some material in this collection that is triggering for survivors of all kinds as well as those who have struggled with infertility, miscarriage, addiction, or suicide. There will be trigger warnings before graphic poems.

Maggie Bowyer
Greensboro, North Carolina
www.maggiebowyer.com
hello@maggiewrites.com

IBSN: 9780578967806
LCCN:

Printed in the United States of America
First Printing, 2021

The Fallen

This book is about eight
Separate love stories,
Probably more, probably
Every soul I've ever
Had the pleasure
Of bumping into.
These might be love stories
But some of them are quite gory,
And other ones could
Have been pure glory.
There are some rugged
Relationships that started
In my infancy, and others
That I destroyed in their infancy.
There are memories I buried,
As well as people,
And while there was a lot
Of heartbreak along the way,
I wouldn't have it any other way.
When I started this journey
To find the child in me,
I found love stories and fairy tales
I had yet to compose in my waking.
I found romance and lessons;
I found a love story that was
Well worth the wait.

I found the bad ones, and
The mostly-good-but
Still-not-the-one, ones.
Then I found you,
And I found myself too.

I knew when I looked into your eyes
There was a new space between us,
Like you were still overseas.
A strangled laugh escaped as I joked -
Choked out, you were going to leave me
Crying in the cafe window seat.
That's when the lightning struck
Across your iris, and the words
Cut me just as quick -
This was it. The goodbye kiss
Then out the door you went.
I should have known the moment
Your lips met mine that we were
Having an affair with borrowed time.
We knew August would come,
And you decided to beat her
To the heartbreak,
Have a great summer break.

He said "I always like the
Happy ones you write."
I almost laughed at the thought,
Purely preposterous.
Sadness is the only thing
That drips from my lips
As naturally as honey;
People love feasting on tragedy.

Kris

She left on a Tuesday.
Why a Tuesday, when I will
Suffer for days before
And days after, bleeding through
Two whole weeks? Months?

It has been years now and she
Still remains, blood stains
Splattered across my brain.
It's not that she was the first
Woman I loved; she was the first
Person I memorialized properly.

She was the first woman
I let myself admit love for.

What for?

Packed up her bags in a week,
Suddenly an airplane is waiting
And I am impatient for that moment
We are alone for a goodbye;
I still have indentations

On my sides from her arms
Wrapped tightly around me.
The way her eyes flashed
Under her eyelashes,
Fearful and tear-full,
Imprinted in my memory.

She flew in on my birthday,
Yet again a Tuesday.
She burst into my classroom
And before I could speak
My legs collapsed on me;
Her arms found their home
Around me, supporting me.

She broke and mended my soul
On a Tuesday.

Thoughts of you swallow me up,
Eat me w(hole),
Larger than the one in my chest.

Bad Trip

I try so hard to reach
The lines as they flutter
From my memory;
It seems the best poems
Always come to me
At the most inconvenient times.
I let my toes slip
Over the edge of my thoughts,
Tumbled down the rabbit hole
Into the forest of memories
(Oh, the way things used
To be so easy; how did they
Feel so impossible back then?)
I am drowning in the past
(But still don't have you back).
I always return from the paper
With more questions
Than reasonable answers.
That's what happens when
You go searching for meaning
Without knowing
What you're looking for.

I am no longer skilled
At making magic
Out of memories;
Instead of symphonies,
They only bring me sadness.

Losing Sight

Originally published in *Bourgeon Online*
This poem may be triggering for those who struggle with addiction

You were the first person
I reached towards,
A single, shaking arm
Plunged into the thick
Fog of fresh grief.
You pulled me through
The first awful snow,
The first month on Earth
Without her;
You pulled me through
Blunt smoke in a stranger's
Bedroom, ash covering
Bedspreads (which we would
Soon spread our bodies against).
You pulled me through
A dissociative dream that was
Spring semester;
Part of me fears
I will be a Junior forever.

You pulled me through
Long class lectures
And unfamiliar hallways.
You pulled me through
Relationships and wreckage,
Much of which, I'll admit,
I created.
You grasped the horns
Of this life with all of your might
(A few too many times),
Until that last night.
Until you were pulled
(A bit too deep)
Into the diseased drugs
Clouding our hometown.
I'm so glad I got out
Alive.
(I'm so sorry I didn't
Have the strength
To pull you through).

Self-Sabotage

I left a birthday bag
On your front porch;
Taped to the inside
Was some semblance
Of a goodbye.
The thunder rocked
My car as I blew through
Puddles on Interstate 85;
I let the rain pour in
Through my open window,
Because breakups always
Call for a smoke, probably two,
Probably twenty before
My wheels deposit me
In my best friend's lawn;
Already soaked to the bone,
Much like my front seat,
I let the freezing drops
Pour over me on their way
To nourishing the same
Grass cradling me.
I tend to make a muck
Of everything I touch,

Didn't want to smudge
Your graffiti heart,
Smear the lines
To the road as we
Hunted for midnight ghosts,
Messy what was already a mosaic;
I knew I would never
Be clean enough to hold you.

Chronically Cursed

The moment I stopped
Loving you
Was the moment I realized
You could not love
The burrito version of me,
Curled up on the couch
With you on FaceTime,
Unable to make a sound.
This disease has taken
Sensuality, spontaneity,
And one day it snatched
The significance
Of our relationship.

I was giving away parts of myself
Before I even knew what they meant.

Your knife
Pierced
My heart,
Leaked
Battery acid
Through
My abdomen;
You carelessly
Tossed a match;
Just as the cigarette
Met your lips,
The little flame
Lit me up.

I haven't been able
To stop putting
The pen to paper
And shredding you,
Desecrating your
Memory.
I can't yet move on;
You haven't stopped
Haunting me,
Now haunting them,
You will haunt her.
I can't watch
As she is torn apart;
I know I'll be there,
In the aftermath.
Someone has to
Remind your victims
They are strong
Once you're gone.
Someone has to
Stop you.
I haven't figured out
Any logistics,

Instead just keep
Crafting and drafting
The plan to end this
Once and for all.

You're stuck in my head
Like rusted pennies
That I can't shake loose
Through my ears filled
With cotton candy lies.

Tell me a story of a girl with cotton candy curls
And a necklace she twirls.

Tell me what made her lavender
Turn so blue. A story of how
A pastel pixie tripped
As she skipped down cobblestone roads,
Chipped her shoulder and heart
On a violent piece of art.

She fell for a red-faced man
With no soul, just a pitch-black hole.

Her long locks used to flow freely
Until his hands ripped hair straight
From her scalp as he pulled her down.

Tell me a story of a girl who's laugh
Used to shimmer as it danced
Its way across the room,

A story of a girl who hasn't smiled
Since her eyes bled black,
Mascara smears her staple fashion statement.

How do I explain that
(Most days) reading
Epic poetry is exhausting;
Cooking dinner is the same
As standing on daggers;
There is danger in every
Step I take lest this fall
Be the one to seal my fate.
The knots in my stomach
Have tangled again;
Passing food through my lips
Has done nothing but
Spike my heart rate
And make the room spin.
I am afraid that things
Are getting bad again.

Breaking news:
You're leaving in the morning.
Can't say that I blame you,
Even though I want to.

Color Blind

Originally published by Poetry 365

Every time I changed my perception
You transformed your deception -
You're a master at disguising
All the bits of your personality
Poking out from your facade.
I always framed things to
Intentionally evade the disgusting
Smirk on your face when a single
Tear dripped from beneath
My rose-tinted, gold-rimmed glasses.
I self-inflicted blindness
To avoid your true colors;
Now darkness is all I see.

I Screamed

Go ahead and leave me then!
Watching you quit
Would be a lot easier than this.

Afterparty

Originally published in *A Cornered Gurl*

After all the guests
Left their fingerprints
On every window
And scuffs up and down
Each hallway,
I searched for you.
I looked underneath
The stacks of jackets
Forgotten by those
Donning flushed cheeks,
Peeked in the guest room,
Let your name shake
Now empty glasses clattering
And cluttering countertops.
They said you slipped out
While I was still dancing;
Now I just have pity parties,
All alone, drinking myself silly.

I only ever meant to be honest,
Not bloody and brutal with my rebuttal,
As if telling you about the absence
You left in the center of my chest
Would do anything but make it wider.

You got to pretend
I was the bad guy,
And walk away.

I'm the only one
Stuck reliving
The trauma.

You got to move on,
Fall in love,
Break more bodies.

I am permanently
Emotionally unavailable
Thanks to you.

I wonder if I sneak in
Through the cracks
In your soul
When you're sleeping.
I wonder if it's
Your daydream
Or nightmare to
Have me show up there.
When you wake up,
With mist already
Clouding your eyes,
Do you tell her
The truth?
Or do you lie
To her too,
Saying
"Darling
I'm only ever
Dreaming of you."

You asked for forgiveness
Without offering
Any repentance.
I watched myself
Snatch your grin
As my lines finally
Sank in.
No matter the future,
These words will always
Follow you.

You Ruined Your Own Reputation

This isn't malicious;
You see these words
As vicious, then why
Can't you understand
This is a simple stand
Against you throwing
Fists through walls
To get what you want.
This is a warning,
To all the girls after me;
Your reputation is on trial,
And I'm not the only witness.
There will be no judge or jury,
This execution is under
Your direct order.
You actions were the spark
That blew us up, so you
Don't get to complain
About where we landed.

Let Them Eat Cake

I forgot today
Is your birthday.

                        Pity.

I would've baked
A decadent cake
Just to smash it
On your car windshield.

To Still Be Naive

I see the glimmer
Still hidden in her eyes;
I've watched it
Fade into the black
Hole you're carving
Through her innocence.
She doesn't even notice.
When will you implode?
Will I be able to
Catch her falling stars?

I couldn't help but notice you've become

I s o l a t e d.

You've retracted your rays of

W a r m t h.

You've pulled the clouds back to cover

S u n l i g h t.

I think everyone is growing more

C o n c e r n e d

As the days keep passing and you're still

A b s e n t.

It's been months since your

F r i (ends)

Have so much as gotten a phone call.
I know you think she's worth your all.

She's not.

I wonder if she
Read my book
About you.
I wonder if you
Sped to all of
The local bookshops
And bought every copy,
Only to light them
On fire.
Are you angry,
Or are you afraid
She will believe me?

I want to shove
These pages
Down your throat.
I want you to
Swallow my pain
Along with your pride.

Devoured

Originally published in *Bourgeon Online*

I just thought you should know
She twists every story into
Something you'd devour
Faster than a piping pretzel.
I thought you deserved to know
She doesn't just crack us like eggs,
She has left half a dozen of us
To rot with our shells shattered.
I thought you deserved a warning:
If you don't run for the exit now,
She will toss you out along with
The leftovers from two weeks ago,
The other ones she forgot about.

I think I'm your
Least favorite ex
Because I stopped
Putting up with your
Bullshit.

I started writing it down.

Eviction Notice

I don't go to
Any of our old
Haunts anymore.
I hardly venture
Beyond my front door.
I don't want to
See you anymore,
Replay the same scene
Over and over.
I refuse to be
A cinema, empty after
All the premier crowds
Have gone and left
Crumpled up napkins
Scattered across me.
I demand more than
Rolled credits,
Cliff hangers without
Promises of a sequel.
I deserve Sundays
Spent on matinees,
Red carpets and
Buttery popcorn buckets.

I want to feel safe
In movie theaters,
And on sidewalks.
I don't need any of
All our old haunts,
I just need you
To stop haunting me.

The Healing

Note to Self

You're not a liar;
You are not the actions
You took in order
To survive.

Amputation

The world got too

Full.

Too crowded,
With strangers' breath
On my neck
On the slowest
Elevator ride of my life.

So many people wanted
To play both sides;
This became black and white
After all those sleepless nights,
Bruises and fights,
Holes in the walls and all.

I elbowed my way through
Throngs of vultures who
Sought out the roadkill
Of my most precious organs.
I burst through the doors,
The wrong floor,

Gasping for fresh air
But still choking -
Anxiety or smog
Hung over me as they stared.

I gutted myself,
Cut myself off from
(Everyone)
(Anyone) who could
Leave me with your stench,
Draw me back in.

This April isn't the Same

The rain bashes against
The window panes, but
This April isn't the same.
The falling drops are colder,
More off-putting,
More like I want to pull
The covers above my eyes
And sleep until summer;
Will the world be any warmer
By June? Is that too soon
To bury all this grief?
Will healing from this take
Seasons rather than months?
Years rather than the few tears
We've shed behind closed doors?
Will we ever have a moment
To mourn this momentous loss?

My therapist had me stand on a balance board,
Watched as I wobbled back and forth.
She wondered if my trauma could alter
The very foundation I stand upon,
If the dizziness of my mind could
Affect my very footing.
She started the timer, 17 seconds
Before I teetered over the edge,
Almost face-planting into an armchair.
Vertigo or the verge of a breakdown,
I have yet to find an experiment
Fit to determine which came first,
The physical or the mental,
Illnesses overwhelm me.

I am going to love myself.

I am growing to love myself.

I Try Not to Mention It

I apologize that this illness is
All my mind can theorize,
Pick apart each zap of pain
As it comes my way.
I hope it doesn't feel like
I keep rewriting the same poem.
It never feels like the same pain.
You never get used to
Your own body attacking you.

All the really
Ugly
Parts of me
Still want the
Few remaining
Beautiful
Parts of you.

There are still days that I wish
You were who I pictured
When the summer sun was fading,
And my cigarette was waning.
I still wonder if there was ever
Anything real that you showed me -
The old ice cream place
In the middle of a field or the tickle
You hid behind your ear;
My greatest fear is nothing
That I know is real.
If I picked up the phone
I'm sure you'd prove me wrong -
At least for another year,
Maybe three.
Or maybe just through dinner
Before you decided
You had to be the winner
(Even if it meant losing me).
I'm sure that you'd be
Perfectly upbeat -
For a week, maybe more,
But maybe less and maybe
This time I wouldn't survive
The final beating.

My body gives my brain
Too much time to complain.

The Last Time

Once I asked you
If you'd still love me
If I got sick.

Of course
I'm not going to leave you.

You were too busy with her
To take ten minutes
To bring me tissues.
You couldn't see the issue.

I started buying
The big bulk boxes
Every time I'm at the store.

I Missed the Lesson

Life is like a simile,
Leaving you wondering
If a metaphor would have
Made this any easier.

I still see my demons
When I catch glimpses
Of my eyes in the mirror.
Recovering from
Lifelong abuse
Is leading me to find
All the fragments of you
I have woven into my armor.
I was only ever trying
To protect myself;
Now I leave gashes
Like kisses
On those who don't
Deserve paper cuts.

I am a reflection of what
You place in front of me
(The worst bits of you).
Can you see right through me?
Does that mean you
Will finally be transparent?
I confuse my identity
When I pull someone close -
I pull on your insecurities
Because they are tethered
To the voice in my head
Calling me pathetic.
My whole life I have been
Obsessed with absorbing
Endless negative energy -
I want to heal the world
Even if I shatter in the process.
I've trapped your words
(And the worst of my relationships)
In the caverns of my cranium.
I need someone to smash
My rock heart to bits,
Rebuild me into a mosaic;
If I'm going to be a mirror,
I want to present the full picture
(And all the beautiful bits).

The wounds
This world
Gave you
Only wove
Magic
Into your armor.

~ The Gospel

You wrapped up
Your broken bits
And left them
On my doorstep
With my Christmas gifts.
I don't think I ever
Properly thanked you
For pulling me out
Of neck-deep waters
Each time my memories
Got ahold of me.
I don't think I ever
Properly apologized
For drowning us
When my demons
Got the best of me.
I wrote this poem
In lieu of a thank you note
I know would only
Benefit me.

I always favored
Saltwater
To pool water.
I always sought clarity,
But waves crashing
On paper cuts snap
My eyes wide open,
Mend the cracked skin.
There is a middle path
In my tepid bath;
I finally decided
Forgiving you
Is really just
Loving myself again.

If I can thank
This disease
For anything,
At least
It brought
My words
Back to me.

I wasn't sure you'd ever
Speak to me again,
So I'm writing another poem
I'll never send.

I don't want to hurt you
The way only I seem to.

I am tired of the
Best friends
Back and forth
Across state lines
And fate's design.

You'd read between my lines,
You'd seen truths I had tried
To deny all my life.

You had read poems
That were tucked
Neatly under my sheets,
Words I never meant
Anyone to read.

You saw inside of me.
Now I only see you
Through phones
And smoke screens;
It's been years since
You've called me
(Your best friend).
My heart aches from knowing
This is how it has to be.

I figured out ten of
The million reasons why
We never worked out.
There's still 999,990
Reasons why I miss
My best friend.

Someone reminded me
Of us the other day,
A casual comment,
"How are they anyway?"
It's been years
Since I thought
Of our tumultuous
Half a lifetime,
Or was it half a year?
Yes, you hurt me dear,
Wounded me in ways
I never made clear
(I usually just disappear).
I'm sorry I didn't stay,
At least to clear the air,
Hear your side.
Years later,
When asked candidly,
"Were those poems about them?"
I answered honestly, *"no."*
That's when I knew
I should write about you.

What, you can't laugh
During sex?

You chuckled into my neck.
I had never felt a touch
So gentle yet piercing -
Reached my core,

Do you feel warm?

Before your hands,
No one had listened
To each of my moans,
Groans and grinds;
Maybe that's why
You are all that is
Filling up my mind,
Even when you aren't
Between my thighs.

Even your calloused
Fingertips paused,
Listened to my heart
Through my skin.

You always knew
When to clear the air,
Pass the smoke
Between our lips,
Because I needed
A moment of silence.

Now the world
Is far too quiet.

To My Best Friend

With us,
It was simple.
It was peaceful.
Thank you,
For being what I needed
When I didn't deserve it.

You were close
But that only counts in
Horseshoes
And hand grenades.
I blew us up
Because I knew you
Weren't the one.
If there was anyone
I would have settled for,
I would be nestled
Next to you right now.
I'm glad we fell short,
Because we both found
So much more.
I hope you're as happy
As I am today.
Love,
Your second place.

I aim to be
Far more than I am.

Maybe that why
I disappoint everyone I love
(Or maybe just myself)
The most.

Bathtubs Can't Replace Friendships

My new best friend
Is far more warm
Than the one before,
Wraps me up in fluid love
That moves to meet me.
When I fill her up,
She pours back into me.
My tears always mix
With her oceans
Therefore I feel no judgment.
I don't have to worry
About oversharing when
I have already taken
The deep dive.
My new best friend
Cannot replace the feeling
Of arms wrapped around me
Or the feeling of air when
Laughter surrounds me.
No matter the warmth,
There will always be
An emptiness when I am
Wrapped in porcelain.

This isn't a death sentence;
Rising up, despite everything
Screaming for you to stay down,
Is how we know we are living.

Brain Spotting

When I was being swept away
In a stream of consciousness,
Icy memories threatening
To chill me to the bone
Before dragging me under,
You were there.
Suddenly, You reminded me
You are always there.
Why do you so
Doubt the talents
I bestowed?
Don't you know
I see all that you have sown,
All you've done to grow?
There is a stillness
In the spring of Your lessons.
There is a moment
When I don't need
Forgiveness
Or validation.
There is a moment
I let myself believe
In myself.

I love you
So much
I whispered to
The tear-stained
Fragile-skinned
Person in the mirror.
I am trying
So hard
To love you.

At first it was
Falling asleep
With my phone
In my hand,
Texting you until
Well past my bedtime.
Now I just
Fall asleep
Next to you.

Golden

Foam sticking to my
Laughing lips, head
Thrown back as my
Hair shakes the magic
Suspended in the air -
The shimmer that
Surrounds you has
Yet to dim; nothing
Can diminish all you
(Have always been)
(Have become)
To me.

Giving people space
Feels like leaving enough room
For my heart to shatter.

Forgive me love,
For pushing you away.
It's no excuse,
But my heart already aches
At the thought of losing you.
Petrified at you lost
From my sights,
I drew arrows to combat
A fictitious future.
I'm sorry I wounded you.

~ I threw my weapons out today

My happiest poems
Have been written
Next to you.

Lover

Your arms are mountains
I ache to climb;
Your eyes are oceans
Full of life
Still undiscovered.
It's a paradise - one
a fool wouldn't fall for,
But I'll stay here
    Anyways.

The Appalling

These words in my brain
Sometimes sound like cats
Begging for their treats
When I open the cabinet.
I'm sorry I'm distracted,
Or a little frustrated,
Irritated;
I can't hold back
My agitation
It's just exacerbating
When the phrasing
So carelessly slips
Between my brain cells
And disappears
In the abyss of best lines
I always forget.

11/9/2016

This campus was once colorful,
People walking by holding hands
With rainbow flags on their backs.
This morning is eerie.
The air feels stale
Rather than still.
No one speaks,
Eyes are hollow
And we are all disconnected.
They ride by on bikes
With black banners billowing
Behind them.
They march down the street
Wearing sheets,
Pointed in their hate.
No one feels safe.
In classes
We remained speechless,
Professors simply taking a seat,
Saying that this moment
Is more important than
Any history we've read before.
The resurgence of hate
Reared its head, enraged.

Pockets of the world
Were waking up;
The beast wanted us to sleep
While he stole the sheep.
We'd long been mourning
The Black children whose
Blood broke in our streets,
But the veil was raised
To reveal babies in cages,
Their mothers forced to drink
Straight from the toilet;
Forcing himself upon
Twenty some-odd women while
He begged white nationalists
For applause through violence.
Darkness caresses our country
As I watch them ride by
With black capes,
Their self-righteous pride.

My windows fog
As I watch frozen
Raindrops bounce
Off ice-cold ground.
I ponder which
Is more frigid
And more fragile:
The iced-over branches
Waiting to be snapped
By a single droplet,
Or my heart trapped
In the cleverly concealed
Glacier growing inside of me?

Soldier

Originally published by *Poetry 365*

I keep pushing through,
Soldiering on as though
This body was not
The only one I possess.
My hands are automated,
My muscles are frustrated.
My hips are bolts
Grinding together,
Until I am stripped
Of my identity,
Until I am nothing left
But a pile of pain.
A skeleton used up,
I gave it all for my country,
Yet capitalism
Never seems to favor
The underpaid laborer.

PMDD, Meet Endometriosis

I'm not sure if I am sitting
In the midst of the worst of it,
The lull before the pain
When you can't feel

a n y t h i n g ,

Or if the worst of it is yet to come,
The days that I feel

e v e r y t h i n g .

Is the worst of it the depression?
When I wallow in the consequences
Of the desolation which I created?
Am I emptied because I tossed out
Everyone I care about?
Or is all of this just anticipation,
The build-up to my own crumbling,
Transformed again into
A weak body on the floor?

Just as the sun begins to rise,
The waves of pain begin to invade.
Every neuron firing inside of me,
Burgundy running down my legs,
Twigs made from splinters
Collected in the dead of winter -
If this crimson keeps bleeding
Through my insides I might not
Make it back to myself in time.

I think my depression burst forth
From my fear of these days.
Depression took hold of an adolescent;
Children can't comprehend
These kinds of bad days,
When your own ligaments
Start to shred your organs,
Rip you apart at your hips
Then snatches your soul
As a keepsake.

Depression won
When the child in me
Had no fight left in them,
Shoved their pain back inside,
Taped up their burned skin,
And tried to pretend
It wasn't still happening.

Depression won when no one
Believed me.

PMDD, Meet Endometriosis

I'm not sure if I am sitting
In the midst of the worst of it,
The lull before the pain
When you can't feel

a n y t h i n g ,

Or if the worst of it is yet to come,
The days that I feel

e v e r y t h i n g .

Is the worst of it the depression?
When I wallow in the consequences
Of the desolation which I created?
Am I emptied because I tossed out
Everyone I care about?
Or is all of this just anticipation,
The build-up to my own crumbling,
Transformed again into
A weak body on the floor?

Just as the sun begins to rise,
The waves of pain begin to invade.
Every neuron firing inside of me,
Burgundy running down my legs,
Twigs made from splinters
Collected in the dead of winter -
If this crimson keeps bleeding
Through my insides, I might not
Make it back to myself in time.

I think my depression burst forth
From my fear of these days.
Depression took hold of an adolescent;
Children can't comprehend
These kinds of bad days,
When your own ligaments
Start to shred your organs,
Rip you apart at your hips
And snatches your soul
As a keepsake.

Depression won
When the child in me
Had no fight left in them,
Shoved their pain back inside,
Taped up their burned skin,
And tried to pretend
It wasn't still happening.

Depression won when no one
Believed me.

Detour Ahead

The laundry was piled
Past my forehead
On your dining room table.
You put a movie about
A stupid horse on TV
While we sat on your little sister's
Twin sized bed, too close
To be comfortable, silence.

He saw the clouds tumble
Over my face when I remembered
The sound of the washing machine
Mixed with the horse's hooves.
I was reading some poem
That mentioned laundry,
And I know my memories should be
Squeaky clean by now
But somehow one line in a book
Transported me to a house
That had long been in a black hole -
How do you fold laundry
In space?

How do we get more space
Between us on this bed,
How do I get light-years
Away from your tongue
Down my throat?
How do I get back
To the right year?

I really am
A sinking ship.
I am not the
Titanic.
There was no
Big send-off
Or rich ladies.
I am the scuffed,
Feared, and torn
Pirate ship.
I am full
Of fools,
Gold lost
A long time ago.
The holes are
Growing wider,
Caverns now
Connecting,
Water overflowing,
And I will do
Nothing.

The Feminist Rant

Originally published in *Word: Volume XIII* (2016)

**This poem may be triggering to survivors of sexual assault
and domestic abuse*

You are finally listening,
Absorbing these words
Originally strung together
By smudged blue ink -
I hope they shock you.

One in every six high school students
In the U.S. is sexually abused
By their partner.

I hope that when I say
I wasn't ready to give you what you took,
Losing parts of me
As easily as baby teeth,
Being cradle robbed,
You understand that each bruise
Is a distinct memory -
How your "jokes" meant
Convincing me you were leaving,

Waiting for me to cry before
You threw out the punch line
And how my punch lines
Only gained me punches to my side;
How I didn't decide yes,
More so I was afraid
Of the fist that never seemed to miss
Or leave a mark;
How even as I beat your shoulder –
Just watch the movie -
Your hands and more
Found places no one had ever been before.

I hope one day you understand
You are not Japan,
And women's bodies are not Nanking
And you cannot just do what you please!

I am now one out of every three high school girls
Around the country
Who has been physically,
Emotionally, or mentally
Abused by my significant other.

I am finally realizing
You were never some musician
To sing me sweetly to sleep,
But rather a poet
With one too many hooks
Embedded in me;
I hope you realize that
Stabs to my ribs
Never stole my voice;

I refuse to become a part
Of the one million
Five thousand women
Who choose not to tell anyone annually.
Instead, I hope that these lines
Rip you apart,
Tear at the seams
Holding your muscles together,
Making you ache the same way
My bloody lips did
Each time you kissed -
Thrusted -
Your thirsty manhood upon me!

I hope that you're sitting there
As ashamed as I was
Lying on your pale blue sheets
Giving up the one thing
I was supposed to hold onto dearly!

I hope you never come home
To your 16-year-old daughter,
Finally seeing all the lies and bruises
Reflected in her pregnancy test,
Hold her shaking form
As she regales to you
Tales of innocence snatching,
Words like *no,*
Please don't,
Not tonight,
Catching in her throat.

This is my way of clearing my throat.

I am a part of the 33% of people
Who name their abuser;
I am joining Emma Sulkowicz
Carrying her mattress
High above her head
At Columbia University,
I am crying out
"Ni una menos"
With all my Latina sisters,
I am standing on this stage,
Regaining my voice,
For the thousands of women
In Dubai who are
Burned alive because
Men treated them as though
They were not worthy of life.
I am standing hand in hand
With the 10% of high school men
Who report being sexually abused.

Can you hear us now?
Can you hear me now?

The Feminist Rant

Originally published in *Word: Volume XIII* (2016)

**This poem may be triggering to survivors of sexual assault
and domestic abuse*

You are finally listening,
Absorbing these words
Originally strung together
By smudged blue ink-
I hope they shock you.

One in every six high school students
In the U.S. is sexually abused
By their partner.

I hope that when I say
I wasn't ready to give you what you took,
Losing parts of me
As easily as baby teeth,
Being cradle robbed,
You understand that each bruise
Is a distinct memory -
How your "jokes" meant
Convincing me you were leaving,

Waiting for me to cry before
You threw out the punch line
And how my punch lines
Only gained me punches to my side;
How I didn't decide yes,
More so I was afraid
Of the fist that never seemed to miss
Or leave a mark;
How even as I beat your shoulder –
Just watch the movie -
Your hands and more
Found places no one had ever been before.

I hope one day you understand
You are not Japan,
And women's bodies are not Nanking
And you cannot just do what you please!

I am now one out of every three high school girls
Around the country
Who has been physically,
Emotionally, or mentally
Abused by my significant other.

I am finally realizing
You were never some musician
To sing me sweetly to sleep,
But rather a poet
With one too many hooks
Embedded in me;
I hope you realize that
Stabs to my ribs
Never stole my voice;

I refuse to become a part
Of the one million
Five thousand women
Who choose not to tell anyone annually.
Instead, I hope that these lines
Rip you apart,
Tear at the seams
Holding your muscles together,
Making you ache the same way
My bloody lips did
Each time you kissed -
Thrusted -
Your thirsty manhood upon me!

I hope that you're sitting there
As ashamed as I was
Lying on your pale blue sheets
Giving up the one thing
I was supposed to hold onto dearly!

I hope you never come home
To your 16-year-old daughter,
Finally seeing all the lies and bruises
Reflected in her pregnancy test,
Hold her shaking form
As she regales to you
Tales of innocence snatching,
Words like *no,*
Please don't,
Not tonight,
Catching in her throat.

This is my way of clearing my throat.

I am a part of the 33% of people
Who names their abuser;
I am joining Emma Sulkowicz
Carrying her mattress
High above her head
At Columbia University,
I am crying out
"Ni una menos"
With all my Latina sisters,
I am standing on this stage,
Regaining my voice,
For the thousands of women
In Dubai who are
Burned alive because
Men treated them as though
They were not worthy of life.
I am standing hand in hand
With the 10% of high school men
Who report being sexually abused.

Can you hear us now?
Can you hear me now?

*This poem may be triggering for some survivors and those
struggling with infertility*

He emptied me
Before he ended me;
He unwrapped his gift
Of domination on top of me.
He peeled back the tape
Holding me together, delicately,
Like he might actually be
Gentle with me tonight.

He ripped into my skin as though
My body was easily discarded,
Like this wasn't the only innocence
I had left to cling to.

I'm left to wonder
If he stole my cradle too,
Robbed me of a future
I now yearn for,
Years down the road.

A Tangled Web

Please don't ask me
Why I still haven't
Gotten a knack
For happy poetry.
I swear I'm trying,
But dammit there
Is still a closet full
Of cobwebs and
Mix-matched
Skeletons
In the back
Of my brain.

I am still trying
To unearth
All of the spiders
And clear out
The dust that
Coats my thoughts
In an inch
Thick layer.

Maybe once
I parse out
Which bones
Belong to which
Corpses of my past,
I will be able
To leave them there.

It's been seven years
And I still feel the ghosts
Of your fingers dance
Their way across my body,
Little flames for their feet.
I still hear your voice
Catching in his throat,
The slightest provocation
Bringing out my imagination.
Is it her scream bouncing
Around my hallway,
Or did I fall asleep again?
I haven't learned the difference
Between visions of his latest victims
And apparitions of who I was back then.
Shouldn't he have been the one
To spend the last seven years
In this impenetrable prison?

You still
Stop me
In my tracks.

You're not
Striking.

You just leave
Everyone
Shell shocked.

Claustrophobia

*This poem may be triggering to survivors of sexual assault
and domestic abuse*

I became a whore
Out of survival.
Have you ever seen
A man with eyes
Filled scarlet,
Beaming carnal energy?
Trapped you in
His bedroom corner,
Sank into your hair
To smell your fear,
Tore you apart
By putting his fist
Through your pussy
And pulling your heart
Out through its teeth?
Propped up on
The bathroom sink,
The first time a man
Made me bleed,
He reached deep
Inside of me,

Drawing roses
Adorned with thorns
As I stared at
The peachy pink
Walls encroaching on me.
I pressed my white fingers
So firmly against the walls,
The vermillion in my knuckles
Began to bleed down them.
I beat the walls but
My palms slipped right off;
I tried to scream
But he shoved my panties
Between my teeth
And threatened me
If I so much as breathed.
So many years later
And I'm still a people pleaser,
Meet and greet with
Your lips between my teeth,
I will grind and sink
Into the pillows or
Bounce towards high heavens,
But I still can't stand
The feeling of walls
Closing in.

I'm still alive
And it's not for
Lack of trying.

I forgot about
The Syngoniums,
Found them
Frostbitten
In the morning.
I know they were
Your favorites,
And I regret
Always losing
My head.
The last place
I recall
Having it on
Was your chest.
Thank you
For forgiveness;
There will be
Far more growth
Next season.

Justice Died

I began shedding layers
As I walked down the city streets;
If anyone saw me, wandering
The winterscape in a white sheet,
They'd mistake me for a spirit.
In reality, I am exhausted from
Lugging around this emotional
Baggage, a griefcase overflowing
With all the paperwork I tried
To file, but a trial never transpired.
Some judge decided my trauma
Was his to determine - as though
He was the one with ghosts
Of hands still on his skin,
As though he was the one who
Bore witness to the worst of it;
The worst part is that it's been
A decade since he touched me
And he's still raping preteens.

I want to run backward
Through time,
To find the 14-year-old me,
To define what words
Like predator mean.
I don't want to learn
The hard way anymore;
I wish I had never learned at all
What it means for a man
To stand over me, smirk pulled
Back tight against his gums,
A full eight feet tall -
I wish I didn't know what fear
Tasted like, but more so I wish
I didn't know what his hands
Tasted like as they shoved their way
Behind my teeth, showing me
That I can still be "sexy"
Even while he's raping me.
There is a part of me still
Digging through thesauruses
In the back of my mind, trying
And miserably failing to define

This gaping hole between my thighs;
I'm still searching for a definition,
A reasoning, a more fitting word
Than "grooming," but most of all
I am desperate to find a way
To report a robbery
Of all the pieces inside of me.

Response

You've formed this
Pack of resentment around me,
This group of people
Clucking their tongues as I pass,
Deeming me a whore,
Complaining about phone call breakups
And cowards.
But do they know?
All of the secrets,
The bottled up envy
You've kept buried in lyrics
Since middle school?
I should tell them,
But instead
I'm planting seeds of agony,
Hoping they'll sprout roots of misfortune,
And maybe the flowers of guilt
Will finally make your insides pretty.
I'm sure they're very angry,
Waiting for provocation
To pounce,

Spread lies like wildflowers,
Stories about the girl
Who hurt herself to be loved,
The whore who
"Gave it up"
On the second date.
My story was already written,
The bruises acting as the plot,
More physical than metaphors
About poets with
One too many hooks
Embedded in me.

I was writing a poem,
Deep in the tangled webs
Of my notes app,
Describing the gorge size
Cuts from my childhood,
When you interrupted,
And maybe I erupted
And if I caused soot
To blanket us in this
Uncomfortable silence,
Suffocating me,
I am incredibly sorry.

I am a relic,
With paper-thin skin
And a heart made from
Whittled down porcelain.
I am sorry that my tongue
Is coated in poison;
I normally hide it
Behind a locked gate
But my pain ate the key
And I am waiting
Until it tears through me
Before I can regain control.

These excuses are flimsy,
A feeble attempt
At keeping you from
Abandoning me.
I will always question
How you've yet to see
I am tattered boundaries
Mixed with broken glass;
I am sharp edges
On a blanket that has
Too many holes
To keep you warm.

No matter how much
I wish I was worth it,
No matter how much
I wish I could lie
And say I deserve love,
I'll never deserve you, love.

Hometown Glory

This poem may be triggering for those who struggle with addiction

The foundation of my childhood
Was built upon heroin needles
And faulty promises;
The only lullaby I learned
Was the sound of car alarms
And cop cars whizzing by.
I long ago lost count
Of all my high school friends
Who went on to
Be just another lost life;
Some of them lie
Beneath our feet
While others lie
In the allies between
Empty showrooms downtown.
We used to crush joints
In the crooks of our fingers
In between classes.
Now my best friend
Is hooked on Percocet;

The worst part is
She doesn't know it yet.
I miss my garage
Smelling like trees;
The house has been empty
Since my mom OD'd.
The town got more dangerous
When the DEA raids started;
Now that all the gangs are packing,
Our town has been popping off
On the nation's most deadly.
Sometimes I wonder why
My memory is fried
Or why my body is in shambles
Or the reasons I'm always high.
At least I got out alive, right?

Stranger Danger was a Strange Lie

This poem may be triggering to survivors of sexual assault

I pause in the doorway,
Right hand still clutched
Around my mace,
My eyes flickering
Back and forth.

I burst in and slam the door
Behind my back, lock
The deadbolt with a quick
Flick of my wrist -
There is fear
Even with familiarity,
Questions on if a stranger,
Or worse (and more likely)
An acquaintance I trusted,
Was lurking in shadows,
Waiting for their moment
To shove their way into
My apartment,
My unwilling bed,
My unwitting head.

Cheers

One minute I was
Surrounded by raised glasses,
Kisses and promises.
We chugged vodka
From water bottles
Like it was the night we met.
Trying to make the best
Of a dimming nation,
I made you my world.
In no time I became
A used-up red solo cup;
I threw myself down
On the dirty bathroom floor
Of a 24-hour diner,
My best friends arms
Around my shoulders;
Your arms already
Draped across her seat;
Which one of us
Already knew it was over?

Heavy

Originally published in *Capsule Stories Autumn 2021*

I've forgotten how to daydream;
These days my mind is constantly
Wondering why my ankles
Won't stop cracking or why
My chest has become so tight,
If it's worth the fight with doctors
Who might just say it's in my head—
Another reason for those I love
To continue to disbelieve me
When it comes down to
All the assistance, understanding
And persistence I might need.
These silences used to mean time
Spent in my mind palace, traversing
A land full of sugar gliders and
Friends made of the wind—
These pauses in between reality
Used to feed my creativity.
Now all my mental space is taken
Up by a pile of medical bills in
Disarray, diagnoses I am unsure
How to explain away, push into

The darkest corners of my brain
Where I can cover them up
With tattered sheets, shame
Blanketing my abilities, or
Lack thereof. These days my mind
Is as fried as the tender skin
Of my abdomen, covered in scars
Created by constantly crushing
Heat into the dried and strung out
Pain-stricken organs beneath.
These days it has become an
Impossible feat to stare out
A window, at ease. These days
There are daggers in my feet
Even as I am resting. These days
There is not a moment of rest,
A second of daydreams, a moment
Of reprieve from this body.

She'll wait for you to dry out
Before she flips you upside down
And hangs you on her wall
Next to all her wilted flowers.

Please

Green was glinting off her iris
In the first picture she posted
With your arms already
Wrapped, still gently,
Around her willing neck.
The forest has since been choked
Out, burnt by fires impossible
For her to stomp out alone.

Standing on the water's edge,
The cliff side's breeze
And your piercing, wolffish gaze
Sliced straight through to bone.
Now and then I wish I had
Jumped right in, head first
Towards the ocean floor.

She is walking a fine line
Between flirty and fun
And a face-first plunge;
Why won't anyone pull her back
Towards safety, warn her

Of the coming storm?
She cannot hear my screams
20 feet beneath the sea.
You all watched as they dug
Into my flesh then tossed me
Over the cliff's edge,
And you know it will happen again;
You're just as hungry for the story
As the wolf is for their prey.

You are red wine,
Purposely spilled
On a summer night;
You probably forgot
How your wrist
So delicately flicked
Cabernet across
My summer best,
A white, flowing dress.
I can't forget the way
You sank into my skin,
Still stained; I see it
Every day as I pull
Still damp clothes
From my body,
All these years later.
The stench comes
In cascading waves,
Devastating my senses
Every time someone
Mentions you were asking
About me again.
I have showered
And soaked
A thousand times
Over (and over)

But I'm not sure
I will ever be able
To wring you out
Of me as easily
As red wine stains
On a white dress.

I've ventured past
The place of the unknown;
I used to wake with the sun,
Lucky to sometimes feel
Rested and wholesome.
As the   Days
                          Months
                          Years
Passed,
I woke up only to realize
Each day brings more
Unyielding pain than the last.
There is no mystery
Left within me,
Only misery.

Insurrection Day

We hold these truths
To be self-evident -
That the white man
Is endowed to be supreme,
And the white woman
Will lurk in his shadow.

This country flies the colors
Of the red white and blue,
Built on the backs of Black bodies,
Our streets still run red
From clashes with the men in blue;
This land has been saturated
With the ravages of my ancestors.
How can we call others
The savages?

We forget our history,
Repeatedly.
We seek higher ground
By standing on broken necks,
Families, whole minorities
We have wrecked.

This melting pot
Has burnt too many;
We might as well burn
This whole country down.

Bigotry

They don't understand translation.
They don't understand transformation.
They don't understand mercy.
They don't understand love.
They don't understand God.

I stood in the middle
Of a four-way stop,
Practically on my knees
As I begged you to stay.
The smirk you wore that day
Represents exactly how
I remember you.
Cocky, and always half-cocked,
You draw a room to you,
Then suck the oxygen
Straight from their lungs.
You're a bait and switch,
I love you's
Slipped between your fists.
The silent treatment
Comes as easily to you
As lying does (and
It almost makes me resent you).
All these memories we shared
Back when love was driving
On a foggy morning,
Now I avoid whole
Swaths of this county.
You blew through a stop sign
Past me yesterday -
It was clear as day.

Blasted through the same
Four-way intersection
I stood in begging for you
A whole year ago.
You barrel through stops signs
And trample on lives -
An unabashed apathy towards
Anyone other than yourself.
I stood on the sidewalk,
Thanked my lucky stars
For looking both ways
And for all your flaws;
If you hadn't broken
Every traffic law
(And piece of my heart),
I might never have realized
How much more
I have always been worth.

Inaugural

Originally published by *Brian Miller Press*

I watched the screen
With my breath held
In between my teeth.
A familiar feeling,
Watching Washington
On another Wednesday.
I waited for the disarray,
The brigade of ostentatious
White supremacy, treason,
The rejection of reality.
Flags waved in place of faces,
A somber day in history;
As they made their promises
And performed their traditions,
I asked God for one commitment:
May we not forget all we have
Learned
    Lost
        Lamented
            Illuminated.

This country's story
Was never ours
To tell.

A Letter to "Missionaries"

They say all these wars
Are over religion; blasphemous.
They are Trojan horses
For white supremacists,
Claiming they're wounded,
Or worse, persecuted.
How are they being oppressed
When they are the ones holding guns
Firmly pressed against foreheads?
This was never about religion.
That's just the easiest vehicle to disguise
Ethnic cleansing and colonialism.

(I break)
Everything I touch
(Turns to gold)

(Porcelain cracked)
Between my fingertips
(Your hair in my grip)

(Did I get too attached to)
This
(Is the only thing
Worth saving
To me)

I had all but convinced myself
I had wilted again,
Until I remembered
Winter has set in.
My leaves may have curled
And turned paper-bag brown,
But my roots are only growing
Deeper and stronger.
Maybe I'll feel better
If it's sunny tomorrow.

Maybe It's Time

I cannot decipher whose insults
Are being hurled through my skull -
These stones reverberate,
Causing damage to my brain.
With every passing minute
I hate myself more - or do I
Really hate you and the torment
You are still putting me through?
You lied
You died
You left me in the diner
Left me standing on the corner
Abandoned me under the streetlight
In the movie theatre parking lot
Disappeared when I needed you the most.
It has become impossible
To know who I am angry at -
The woman who raised me,
The abusers who made me,
Or maybe I wish I could pull
Your words from my voice,
Finally lay to rest the insecurities
You all buried in me.

The Godly

The depression is a crushing fear
That feels just like the air, charged
And packed with pressure before
The sky falls out, all over me.
The depression lurks, waiting
For the moment I lose my vigilance,
For the morning my bones
Are too heavy to lift in the shower,
Wash the night sweats off;
The depression tells me not to worry
That today is the third day
I have sat on the side of my tub,
Watching as the shower washes
Straight down the drain, clean without me.
The towel on my skin rubs and chafes,
Pushes me back towards blankets,
Plush piled high on the bed before me.
Then she hugs me, the first warm touch
My mind can recall - time slips
Out the door when depression enters;
6 months later and I am emerging
From the depths of my lair.
Please be forgiving, delicate
With the monster depression
Has discreetly twisted me into.

My mind is a very dark place;
I guess that's why I try to
Rewrite the world
With beautiful words.

We, the Prose

God must have
Been a poet,
A lonely one
At that.
They crafted
Storylines
But, like any
Good poet,
The speaker
Overpowered Them.
Our mistakes are
Works of art;
Our choices
Are poetic justice.
God was simply
Restless -
We are products
Of a wandering soul
And dancing hands;
We are the gifts.

Perfection
Is my worst enemy,
Spending all my
Precious energy
Searching for
The next peak.
Perfection twirls me
Like a spinning top
On a balcony;
Everyone watches,
Bated breath,
Intoxicated until
Disoriented.
Perfectionism is chasing
The spinning top
Off the nearest ledge.
Perfectionism is
Still spinning
On the way down.

None of us
Survive
All the way
To adulthood
Without first being
Killed a thousand
Little ways.

I have finally dug
Beneath all the gore
Of my relationships before.
Underneath a heap of
Memories on their way
To be donated,
Pages already written, was
Something long kept hidden,
My personal treasury:

How he used to comfort me when
Flashbacks overwhelmed me
In sophomore biology;

How she smiled when I pulled
A new little black dress
And a bottle 'blood orange' liqueur
From my party bag;

How it felt to be held tight
On Halloween night, camped
Out in the trunk of my SUV.

Adolescent pranks
And the most agonizing
Forms of love followed us
All the way here.

It has taken ten years
To sift through all the regret
To find the parts of youth
That are worth holding onto.

Seven

I don't think
I said goodbye.
When you're having
Sleepovers now,
Does your wild hair
Get tangled
In someone else's
Hands?

Puppy Love

Do you remember when
We found your brother's
Dirty magazines
Under the bathroom sink?
Or when I folded myself
Into the washing machine
When we were playing
An epic game of hide and seek?
Do you remember
Late nights in your lawn
With a flashlight
Chasing fireflies?
(Charlotte) sometimes I wonder
Where you are,
And if wherever you are,
You think of me.
I still feel my fingers
Tangled in your blonde mane;
When I squint I can
Even see your speckled,
Freckle-covered face.
What do you remember
When you think of me?

I hope you remember
The times my cheeks
Turned a flushed pink,
Matching your sheets,
When you'd get close to me.
(Did we pretend we were
Best friends
Because we didn't know
What else we could have been?)

Printworks Bistro

Originally published in *Blooming Scribe* (2014)
Published in *Germ Magazine* (2014)

We went to the thrift store
And found the most magnificent dress,
Black and tight
Hitting you at mid-thigh,
See-through sleeves snaked down to your wrists.
It was on sale,
Only $21.
Later I snuck back
And bought it
Because I wanted to take you for dessert
At your favorite restaurant.
You ate so slowly,
Sipping at espresso
Even though it was already 8:30.
I tapped my foot
Rapidly against your stiletto toes,
Because the only reason
I had dug $21 dollars out of my pockets
Was to see you come home
Slightly giddy from our late night snack,
Watch you peel off those lacy sleeves,

Slide your way out of that dress,
Sit on the edge of my bed
And complain to me about your aching feet;
Then I can shake my head
And hand you a ratty T-shirt
Promoting a diner long foreclosed,
And you'll slip your toes and bare legs
Under my pile of blankets.
You'll wrap yourself around me
Just so you can fall asleep.
In the middle of the night
You'll wake up to tell me to turn the heater off,
Turn out the light,
And just go to bed already.
That was the image I wanted to see
When I bought you a dress
Overly revealing.

I Still Drive by Your Old House

Everyone else walked out
To wait in the front yard.

We were standing face-to-face
For one of the last times.
You grabbed my wrist
Just to tug me into a gasp
Of a hug, as though we were
Sharing the last bit of oxygen on Earth.
There was a certain breathlessness
As I tugged you a little closer
Before the moment passed.

They are still waiting.

I pulled on your suitcase
Without letting my hand
Drop from your waist.
I wouldn't waste
Our last moments
Pretending.

We can't keep them waiting.

I used to hide your name
In my line breaks -
When you left town,
I reached out through
Smokescreens and similes.
I used to hide myself,
Placed the truth delicately
Within my pining,
A secret only sapphics
Would decipher -
When I wrote about flowers,
I was describing the way the breeze
Caught each strand of your hair
In the sun's gaze;
When I went on about the wind,
It was an attempt to capture
Your scent
Mixed with the ocean breeze
That one week you
Went away with me.
Teasing and testing me,
You let clear water ripple
Around your naked form,
In front of me for the first time.
Your whispers sent shivers
Through my shoulders,

Years spent yearning enough
To override my senses.
There were no tide pools
Deep enough to prepare me
For your beauty as the moon
Threw shadows across your face;
I wish I had been brave enough
To dive straight in back then.
A few years and states away;
The months blur together now,
The moon cycles shifting
Seemingly faster every time.
I wonder if you dare
Ask yourself, *what if?*
When you see her,
Full and bright above you.

Gratitude

Sunset and summer skies,
You told me you'd leave that night.
I promised I'd visit you
But that was just an excuse
Not to kiss you at the airport.
I was never sure if I was afraid
Of giving away pieces of myself
Or if I knew God had created
Soulmates for a reason
And I just hadn't met mine yet.
If I had kissed you that day,
I might have followed you
All the way across the country;
Now my love lives on its own
Paradise Island.

My Gender *is* Art

They asked me why
I never tried to use this medium
To describe the art
That is my gender;
This work lives to depict itself,
Or to forget the concept exists.
More than performance art,
Yet desires no main stage,
This art has to be lived.
My gender cannot be wrapped up
In simple sentences,
Nor does it wish to be reduced
To art that will be consumed,
But maybe they're right;
Maybe I'll give it a try.

Coach Said

If you don't write your own story
Someone else will write it for you.

I remember this kid in my writing class
Signed my yearbook *'You totally*
could be another Sylvia Plath,
but please don't put your head
in an oven.
     Endings suck.
       K bye!'

I remembering thinking *"What*
A fucking dare,
     I might just do it."

My dad said I should come
With a warning label
'Independent,
     To a fault.'

But he also said he was teaching me
To be the perfect wife, not just
Loving football, but knowing the rules too,
Not just outdoorsy for the tan,
But to sweat up the mountain,
Pee at the top, and make dad jokes
About falling off a cliffside.

I fell out of womanhood,
Clung to the branches of nonbinary,
Called myself a tomboy,
Stuck my head in the oven
And burnt myself out of the binary,
Finally killed the part of myself
That people referred to as *her.*

Identity

Mystifying, the way a pronoun
Can transform into a noun,
The sweater around my shoulders
As the sun sinks to the ground.

Transcendence

I still remember
How you and your mama
Would scream over
A pot of roast,
How she raked you
Over the coals.
I hope one day
She accepts you,
And if she's gone
Before she can,
Please know I still do.
Please know
I still pray for you;
I hope she's fallen
From her high horse
If she's with a higher power.
I hope she's looking down
And thinking she's proud,
About how she missed out.
I know that she liked me
Because she didn't mutter
'Bitch' in Bosnian
Under her breath
Whenever I slept over;

I hope she grew to like
All of you, too.
If she never did,
Know that I always knew,
And never stopped
Loving *you*.

The silence screamed
As she sat across from me.
Puckered lips were masked quick
By a placid smile and a question

You still have a boyfriend though,
Right?

As though I could answer incorrectly
About my own identity.
The silence crept back in and we
Never spoke of it again.
She turned a passive (aggressive)
Cheek, like anyone else
Who was ever blood to her.
I would never be accepted,
But it was a sticky feeling
To not be outright rejected.

She was gone before I was ready
To have a direct conversation,
Before I shared the truest parts
Of who I had always been;
When I sat in front of her,
A waxy figure, there was a hollow
Feeling within both of us.

The tears rolled rapidly down my cheeks.
I prayed to God that she would see
That my identity is the truest
Manifestation of Their image
That I can imagine;
We are heaven-sent.

I pray for my boundless siblings;
I pray their parents realize,
See divine acceptance, that
God would lift the veil of hatred
And their parents would all
Stand in amazement.
The godliest things inside us
Burst forth with authenticity;
Heaven has no limits,
God only wants you to know
How special,
How perfectly right,
You have always been.
Know even if the world
Never swallows their ignorance
And replaces it with pride -
I love you.
I am sorry,
And I love you.

I wonder if those of us
Who disappear,
Unwillingly,
Are the Spirit.

Best Friend

When I look up at the sky
Late into the night,
The moon only a sliver,
I can still see a silver string
Of sparkles connecting each
Of the stars to one another,
The same way our memories
Connect us infinitely.
The warm summer air
Mixed with our cigarette smoke
As we ran across the highway -
I don't know if it was the late hour
Or the psychedelic's power,
But I had full faith as we burst
Across the lanes, the hair in our faces
Only pulled back by our laughter.
We always had a taste for adventure,
Tucked it underneath our tongues
In order to bury our grief;
I no longer get blasts from the past
Randomly when I crack my back,
But I am not sure I will ever see
The stars, or life,
The same since I met you.

Mushroom Magic

I've met God
A few times now.
They're kind with
Big brown locks
Piling naturally
Atop Them
Like a crown,
And a smile
Made of a thousand
Stars.

Cycles

Just yesterday I thought
You had gone missing -
Reported you were gone
After the first 48 hours
But nothing was done about it;
I feel foolish now, with you
On my doorstep, looking up
With your irresistible gaze
Whispering these poems in my ears,
Pouring from my palms through my pen.
I should have known you would
Always come back home.

Inspiration

She holds out her palm,
Expectant, waiting, however
Impatiently, for me to spit
A little bit of soul out for her.
She is demanding, never
Placated by mountain ranges,
Views and taking my time;
She is always running, full
Speed down some hillside,
Dragging me along at her side.
We trip over indecision,
Attempt to ditch grief
As we dodge other people's
Feelings like landmines.
She has tunnel vision,
Trying to help me handle my emotions
More head-on, but sometimes
She needs a bit of my direction.
We are through the worst of it
Before I even realize I am writing;
Sometimes I find random poems
Tucked in my sock drawer
Or frozen in my ice-cube tray,

And I wonder who wrote such
Mind-snapping, soul-bending
Recipes for magic;
Sometimes I wonder if inspiration
Has a few souls she bounces between
When she is lonely, and I am lucky
Enough she has found a home in me.

I lie on the bathroom floor,
Atop rugs that tug at the nerves,
I curse in my face.
God, where is the grace?
Were you under the impression
That I was invincible?
Just because you dropped me
Time and time again,
Doesn't mean I'll never break.
They led me towards
My childhood cure;
They filled the kettle,
Started a bath,
And called my love home.
I sank into the tub,
Quite surprised at the oats
Filling it to the brim,
My childhood friend.
Grace is given in remembrance,
In learning from the past,
Through perseverance.

I have woven
Magic
Into your armor;
You see the pain,
The shimmering
Of sharp edges,
But never the very
Things that makes you
Mystical.

~ my child

I have woven
Magic
Into your armor;
You see the pain,
The shimmering
Of sharp edges,
But never the very
Things that make you
Mystical.

~ my child

Medicating

I don't want to defend
My dependency -
Yes, I'm needy
(Or maybe really
In need).

There is always a moment
We think we can save them.
Walk in only to leap forward,
Spring into action to get
Any sort of reaction.
There was a moment
After your final moment;
The moment that I was
The only one holding the grief,
When no one knew you were gone
Except for me.
I can never unsee
Pain laid out on the mattress,
Grief of the last battle
In a long, invisible war.

It is not your fault.
You have fought hard
Through a battle that
Many mighty have lost.
You are not a failure.

In this moment,
And every moment
Moving forward,
You are important.
You are cared for.

Suicide is an experience
No party involved
Is ever prepared for.

Is it truly unproductive
To live in a body that is
Simply fighting to exist?
What about this art,
A true labor of love?
On (all of) my (worst) days,
These words are my lifeline -
What is that worthy of?

   - What am I Worthy of?

Faith

I'm not sure I'll ever have the answers
To life's greatest questions, but
Maybe that's the problem;
Why am I trying to solve it?
Shouldn't I just live it?
There isn't a cheat sheet
Because no one else has been
Beyond this very moment;
How could they know the answer
To a question that's never been posed?
How can any of us know,
With any level of certainty
What lies beyond this?

I have been drowning
For eons;
I forgot how Your voice
Sounds underwater.
I forgot how Your voice
Leads me homeward.
Give me mercy, Father;
Warm my bones, Mother;
Heal my soul, Redeemer;
Calm my fears, Protector.

Chosen Family

Months had passed
Since I had last
Stepped into Your home.
Timid, I folded myself
Inward at the sight
Of outstretched hands,
Fearful of staining them.
He said
"I am here to mend
The wounds
Religion has left in you."
He questioned,
"If God is a parent,
Why are you always afraid
They will punish you?"
"Maybe I need to tend
To the scorches
Family has left in me."

One Sunday his sermon
Hit a little too close to home
And I thought
Maybe I should've never
Let my walls crumble

To an outstretched hand.
"I've got to get out of here"
I whispered, and then I ran;
I never get very far
When I let emotion
Cloud my vision.
She found me, tear-stained,
Sulking in my car,
Looking up at the steeple.

"I wonder if it's high enough,
Or not far enough of a leap."
She pondered, as though
She could hear me thinking.

"You don't have to join us today;
We will be here when you're ready.
Here's $5; go grab a coffee,
On me."

"I promise, I'll be back."
And I swear to God I meant it.

Maggie Bowyer (they/them/theirs) is a poet, cat parent, and the author of *The Whole Story* (Margaret Bowyer, 2020) and *When I Bleed: Poems about Endometriosis* (2021). They are a blogger and essayist with a focus on Endometriosis and chronic pain. They have been featured in Bourgeon Magazine, Capsule Stories, Detour Ahead, Written Tales, Scribe, and more. They were the Editor-in-Chief of The Lariat Newspaper, a quarter-finalist at Brave New Voices 2016, and they were a Marilyn Miller Poet Laureate.